THE WORLD OF
BIRTHDAYS

Paula S. Wallace

Gareth Stevens Publishing
A WORLD ALMANAC EDUCATION GROUP COMPANY

Please visit our web site at: www.garethstevens.com
For a free color catalog describing Gareth Stevens Publishing's list of high-quality books
and multimedia programs, call 1-800-542-2595 (USA) or 1-800-387-3178 (Canada).
Gareth Stevens Publishing's fax: (414) 332-3567.

Library of Congress Cataloging-in-Publication Data

Wallace, Paula S.
    The world of birthdays / by Paula S. Wallace.
        p. cm. — (Life around the world)
    Summary: Discusses how birthdays are celebrated in Australia, Brazil, Egypt, Germany, India,
Japan, Mexico, Russia, South Africa, and the United States. Includes instructions for making
a craft, game, or recipe from each country.
    Includes bibliographical references and index.
    ISBN 0-8368-3659-6 (lib. bdg.)
    1. Birthdays—Juvenile literature. [1. Birthdays.] I. Title.
GT2430.W35   2003
394.2—dc21   2002191111

First published in 2003 by
Gareth Stevens Publishing
A World Almanac Education Group Company
330 West Olive Street, Suite 100
Milwaukee, Wisconsin 53212 USA

Produced by Design Press, a division of the Savannah College of Art and Design.
Designers: Janice Shay, Maria Angela Rojas, Andrea Messina.
Editors/Researchers: Gwen Strauss, Nancy Axelrad, Lisa Bahlinger,
 Susan Smits, Cameron Spencer, Elizabeth Hudson-Goff.

Gareth Stevens editor: JoAnn Early Macken
Gareth Stevens designer: Tammy Gruenewald

Photo Credits
Corbis: /Stephanie Maze, page 11; /Dean Conger, page 35; /David Turnley, cover, page 39.
Getty Images: /Julia Fishkin, page 13; /Guido Alberto Rossi, page 15; /Stephen Wilkes, page 23;
 /Digital Vision, page 43.
Index Stock Imagery: /Lonnie Duka, page 7.
Masterfile: /Roy Ooms, cover, page 18.
Picture Quest: /PhotoDisc/C Squared Studios, page 34.
SuperStock: /Steve Vidler, cover, pages 19, 27, 31.
Additional photography by Campus Photography, Savannah College of Art and Design.

Illustration Credits
Hui-Mei Pan: pages 8, 9, 10 bottom, 16, 17, 22, 24, 25, 26, 28, 29, 32, 33, 40, 41, 42 bottom.
Angela Rojas: page 21.
Katherine Sandoz: pages 6, 10 top, 14, 18, 30, 34, 38, 42 top, 44, 45.

Printed in the United States of America

1 2 3 4 5 6 7 8 9 07 06 05 04 03

CONTENTS

Words that appear in the glossary are printed in
boldface type the first time they occur in the text.

This little book of birthday traditions is a celebration of the many wonderful ways the world says "Happy Birthday." Everyone has this special day, but not everyone celebrates it the same way. Children in Russia pin their party favors to a clothesline. In Japan, people eat a special meal of sweet rice with red beans. In Mexico, young people share Three Milk Cake and break a piñata full of candy.

Since the 1940s, the world has become a smaller place. The influence of American-style birthdays has altered the traditional customs of many nations, some of which had not formally celebrated birthdays. Yet, even in countries that have assumed the Western traditions of cake, balloons, and presents, many lovely differences between cultures remain. Every day, somewhere, candles are lit and blown out, wishes are made, doves are released, a feast is shared, and salt is scattered. People greet each other in hundreds of languages and show their love and friendship. In every place, in many ways, it's a great day to have a birthday!

 Note: *Whenever you see this sign, you must ask a grown-up for help.*

 **Note:** *Whenever you see this sign, you will need to use a photocopy machine.*

AUSTRALIA

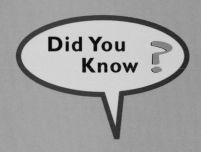

Because Australia is located below the equator, it is often referred to as "Down Under."

Many Australian birthday parties are barbecues because the climate is mild. Even most winters are not very cold.

The **Aborigines** (ab-uh-RIJ-uh-nees), or native Australians, still speak about thirty different languages. Today, however, most Australians speak English, so they wish each other "Happy Birthday," just as people do in other English-speaking lands. Most of Australia's first **immigrants** came from England, so many Australian traditions are English. Today's Australians come from many different countries and cultures. Families bring their own special ways of celebrating birthdays and other holidays with them from their native countries.

Fairy bread is a popular snack in Australia. It is buttered bread covered with tiny candies that children in the United States call "sprinkles." In Australia, children call the candies "hundreds and thousands."

Koalas

A koala is a marsupial mammal, which means that, as a baby, it grows in its mother's pouch and feeds on her milk. *Koala* is an Aboriginal word for "no drink." Koalas don't drink water because they get enough moisture from the eucalyptus leaves they eat. The koala is found only in southeastern Australia. Another marsupial mammal native to Australia is the red kangaroo. Both baby koalas and baby kangaroos are called "joeys."

How to make
Fairy Bread

You will need:
- cookie cutters
- butter knife

Ingredients:

slices of fresh bread

softened butter

hundreds and thousands

   (multicolored candy sprinkles)

Cut slices of bread into fun shapes with cookie cutters. Spread butter on the bread. Top with hundreds and thousands. Gobble it up!

How to make a
Lunch Bag Puppet

You will need:
- markers or crayons
- scissors
- glue
- lunch-size paper bag

❶ Photocopy the koala shapes (opposite page).

❷ Color the face, ears, and legs.

❸ Carefully cut out the colored shapes.

❹ Glue the face and ears onto the bottom of the paper bag (as shown). Glue the legs onto the bag near the opening (as shown). Enjoy your hand puppet from Down Under!

(ear)

(legs)

(ear)

(face)

9

BRAZIL

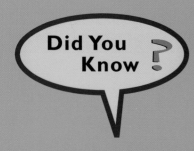

In Brazil, school friends pull the birthday child's ears, for luck, and crack an egg on his or her head as a symbol of new birth!

When you are a birthday guest at a Brazilian's home, you should kiss the side of your index finger, then pinch your earlobe between the same finger and your thumb to show that you enjoyed the meal.

Birthday foods in this South American country include *bolo de laranja* (BOH-loh jee la-RAHN-jah), which is orange cake; **marzipan**, which is candy shaped like fruits; *bridadeiro* (bree-jah-JAY-roh), which is a chocolate ball; and ambrosia, which is sliced oranges with coconut sprinkles. Another favorite treat is coconut candy wrapped in colored paper. Sweet treats are called *docinhos* (doh-SEE-nyos). *Salgadinhos* (sow-GAH-jee-nyos) are small, spicy appetizers.

How to make Bolo de Laranja

You will need:
- **Bundt or tube pan**
- **measuring cups**
- **measuring spoons**
- **mixing bowls**
- **wooden spoons**
- **knife or spatula**
- **serving plate or cake plate**

Ingredients:

vegetable cooking spray

flour

one box of yellow or white cake mix

orange juice

vegetable oil

eggs

Glaze:

1 cup (110 grams) powdered sugar

3 tablespoons orange juice

1/4 teaspoon vanilla extract

Spray the Bundt or tube pan with vegetable cooking spray. (Do not use a layer cake pan.) Dust the pan with flour. Mix the cake according to the directions on the box, but use orange juice instead of water. Pour the cake batter into the tube pan and bake it according to the directions on the box. When the cake has cooled but is still warm (about 10 minutes), loosen it from the sides of the pan with a knife or a spatula. Place a serving plate over the cake and turn the tube pan and the plate upside down at the same time. The cake will settle onto the plate.

Mix together the powdered sugar, orange juice, and vanilla extract in a clean bowl. Slowly pour the glaze over the warm cake.

How to play **Peteca**

The popular game *peteca* (peh-TEH-kah) was played hundreds of years ago by Native people in South America. Today, it can be played by teams of twelve players, with a net and a **shuttlecock**, or by as few as two players, with a beanbag.

Children in Brazil like to play this version of peteca at parties. The first player throws the beanbag into the air and bats it upward with one hand. While the player keeps batting the bag into the air, he or she recites the alphabet. If the bag falls to the ground before the player gets to Z, the next player picks it up and starts batting it. The player who says the most letters of the alphabet without letting the beanbag fall to the ground wins.

    Can you can make it to Z? Try counting!

13

EGYPT

Did You Know?

In the fourteenth century B.C., King Tutankhamen, also known today as "King Tut," became the ruler of Egypt when he was about nine years old. He ruled until his death at about age twenty.

The most popular pets in ancient Egypt were cats.

Ancient Egyptians thought a toothache could be cured by eating fried mice.

When an Egyptian baby is one week old, he or she is laid on a special mat on the floor. The baby's mother then steps carefully back and forth over her child to **symbolize** lifelong protection. Neighbors throw salt in the air for good luck.

A child's first birthday party includes a lot of dancing and singing. Flowers and fruit, which are symbols of life and growth, are used to decorate. So many guests and family members celebrate that, often, two birthday cakes are served, one with candles and one without. Party guests also eat small sandwiches on French bread, sesame sticks, and *kerfa metka-hala* (CAIR-fuh met-KAH-hah-lah), which is hot milk with cinnamon.

Children like to make a decoration called a *zeena* (SEEN-ah), which is a garland made of bright paper cutouts that look like flowers.

How to make a **Zeena**

You will need:

- **brightly colored sheets of lightweight paper, 8½ x 11 inches (22 x 28 centimeters)**
- **scissors**
- **stapler**
- **clear tape**

pattern

❶ Starting with the short side, fold the paper back and forth as if you were making a fan. Make the folds about 1 inch (2.5 cm) wide. You should have about eight folds.

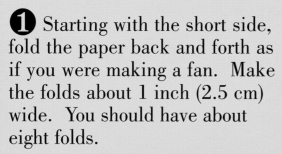

❷ Bend the folded paper in half to mark the center, then open it again.

 ❸ Photocopy the pattern above, enlarging it to fit your paper.

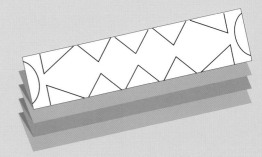

❹ Hold the pattern together with the folded paper. Cut carefully along the lines.

5 The cut paper will look something like this. Staple the center together.

6 Stretch the ends of the top fold of the paper around to meet each other and tape them together. Then stretch the ends of the bottom fold around and tape them together.

7 You should have a finished flower that looks something like this.

8 Make several more zeena flowers in bright colors. Tape them together and hang them on the wall for decoration.

GERMANY

Did You Know ❓

The tradition of putting candles on a birthday cake began in Germany. It started with the ancient practice of honoring gods with torches and candles.

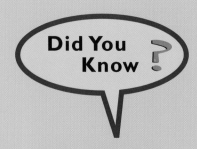

Birthday parties began in Germany two hundred years ago with *Kinderfeste* (KEEN-dahr-FESS-tuh), which means "child's feast" in German. In those days, the birthday child was treated to a **marionette** show.

Today, German children still celebrate birthdays in a special way. The house is decorated, and the dining table has a special wreath placed upon it. A child gets gifts in the morning, a holiday from homework and household chores, and an evening feast. During the feast, the child lights a Life Candle. This candle is given to the child when he or she is a baby, and it is lit once a year on each birthday until the child turns twelve. With each passing year, the candle becomes smaller as the child grows taller!

Birthday treats in Germany include *butterkuchen* (BUH-tair-KOO-kin), or butter cake; *pfeffernuesse* (fay-fur-NEW-zuh), or spicy cookies; and fruit punch.

How to make **Butterkuchen**

Ingredients:

1 package hot roll mix
  plus all ingredients
  called for on the package

1 teaspoon natural
  lemon extract

$1/4$ cup (55 g) sugar

1 extra egg

vegetable cooking spray

Butter Topping:

1 cup (220 g) sugar

1 teaspoon cinnamon

1 stick (110 g) butter

$1/3$ cup (50 g) blanched
  and slivered almonds

You will need:

- measuring cups
- measuring spoons
- mixing bowls
- wooden spoon
- baking pan,
  9- x 13-inch
  (23- x 33-cm)
- small towel
- knife or fork

 Ask a grown-up to preheat the oven to 375° Fahrenheit (190° Celsius). Follow the directions on the roll mix package. Add the lemon extract, the sugar, and the extra egg to the roll batter. Stir all ingredients until smooth.

Grease the baking pan. Pour the roll batter into the pan and spread it out evenly. Cover the pan with a towel and let the batter sit for 45 minutes. The batter will rise.

To make the butter topping, mix the sugar and cinnamon in a small bowl. Ask a grown-up to help you cut the butter into small pieces. With very clean fingers, rub the butter into the cinnamon and sugar until balls the size of peas form. Sprinkle the butter topping and the almonds over the batter. Bake for 25 to 30 minutes or until the top of the butterkuchen is golden brown and syrupy.

How to make a **Life Candle**

You will need:
- sheets of colored beeswax
- tiny cookie cutters
- large white pillar candle that can stand on its own
- thin permanent marker in a dark color (black, purple, or blue)

❶ To form shapes by hand, tear off tiny pieces of the beeswax and warm them in your hand so that they soften. Shape the beeswax the same way you would shape clay. You can make stars, hearts, flowers, or trees. Try to keep the shapes flat.

❷ Use the cookie cutters to cut shapes into the sheets of beeswax.

❸ While the beeswax is still warm and soft, press the shapes onto the candle.

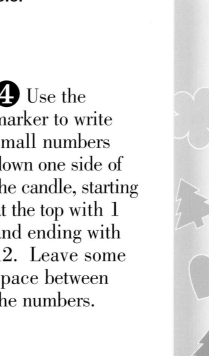

❹ Use the marker to write small numbers down one side of the candle, starting at the top with 1 and ending with 12. Leave some space between the numbers.

❺ Light the candle on each birthday and let it burn down to the next number. As the candle melts, the decorations will slowly melt with it.

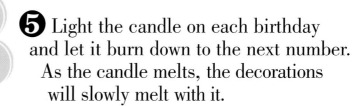

21

INDIA

Did You Know ?

Shadow puppets are popular throughout India. Puppeteers put on shows in village squares for special occasions, such as birthdays or weddings. To create the shadows, the puppeteers perform behind a sheet that is hanging from bamboo poles.

The game of chess was invented in India.

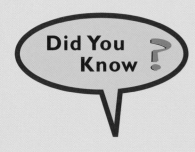

Many Hindu families in India celebrate important Samskaras, or **sacraments**, at different points of life. Samskaras include Jatakarma (JOT-ah-CAR-mah), or childbirth, when a new baby is welcomed into a family; Chudakarma (CHEW-dah-CAR-mah), the first haircut, at the age of one or three years old; and Karnavedha (CAR-nah-VAYD-ah), which is an ear piercing on the third or fifth birthday. The Hindu custom is to celebrate birthdays until a child is sixteen years old. After that age, children are considered too old for parties.

In India, some birthday celebrations are quiet and religious. The birthday child wakes up early, dresses in new clothes, and kneels to touch his or her parents' feet as a sign of respect. The family then visits a religious **shrine** together. They offer a gift of flowers to the gods, and the child is blessed. A priest marks the child's forehead with red or black dye to show that the child has received a birthday blessing. In the afternoon, the family enjoys a birthday feast!

How to make **Shadow Puppets**

You will need:
- **glue**
- **heavy paper or poster board**
- **scissors**
- **flashlight**

❶ Photocopy and enlarge the shapes on this page or draw your own puppet shapes.

❷ Glue the shapes onto the heavy paper or poster board.

❸ Cut out the shapes.

❹ When you have made as many shapes as you want, turn off the lights and hold the shapes up in front of a wall. Shine a flashlight behind the shapes to cast shadows on the wall.

❺ Put on a play, act out funny skits, or make your shadow puppets dance. You can be a puppeteer!

JAPAN

Did You Know?

Making loud, gulping sounds when you drink is customary in Japan!

Origami is the Japanese art of folding squares of paper into shapes that look like animals, flowers, or other objects.

According to Japanese tradition, a baby boy at thirty-two days old or a baby girl at thirty-three days old is taken to a **Shinto** (SHEEN-toh) priest to be blessed. After the blessing, the child receives toy dogs from relatives and friends to symbolize good health.

Each November 15, for Shichigosan (SHEE-chee-goh-sahn), or the Seven-five-three Festival, three- and five-year-old boys and three- and seven-year-old girls dress up in their best clothes and visit a Shinto shrine to celebrate their growth. At the shrine, they pray and have their photographs taken. Girls wear traditional Japanese *kimonos* (kee-MOH-nohs).

Seijin no hi (SAY-jin noh hee), or Coming-of-Age Day, is celebrated nationally in Japan in January. Everyone who will be twenty years old during the year celebrates with feasting and **karaoke** singing.

Hanetsuki

To play the popular Japanese birthday game *Hanetsuki* (ha-nay-TSOO-key), you need four or more players and two or more large balloons filled with air. Players form equal-sized teams. Each team takes one balloon and forms a circle. When a signal is given, a player from each team bats a balloon into the air. Using only their open hands, players try to keep their team's balloon in the air the longest to win the game.

26

How to make an
Origami Samurai Helmet

You will need:
- **one sheet of colored paper, 9 x 9 inches (23 x 23 cm) square**

❶ Fold the paper in half to form a triangle.

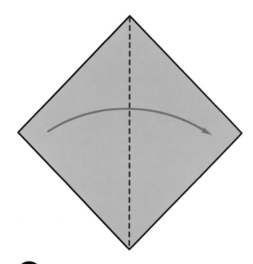

❷ With the triangle pointing downward, fold each side point down to the center point, forming two new triangles, side by side.

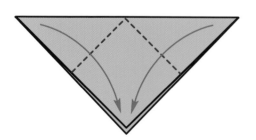

❸ Fold each of the new triangles in half by folding the bottom points upward. You should now have a diamond shape with two small triangles on the top and a large triangle on the bottom.

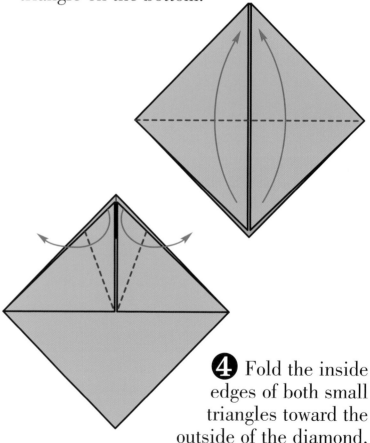

❹ Fold the inside edges of both small triangles toward the outside of the diamond.

❺ Fold the top layer of the large bottom triangle partway up.

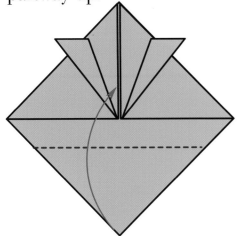

❻ Fold the top layer up again at the fold line between the top and bottom triangles.

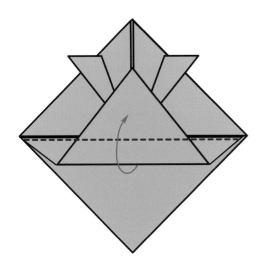

❼ Fold the two outside corners of the diamond shape back behind the diamond.

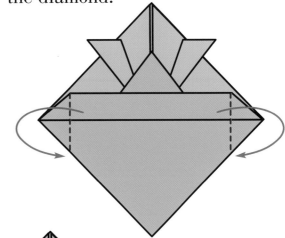

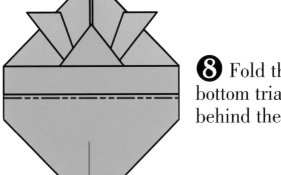

❽ Fold the remaining bottom triangle back behind the top triangles.

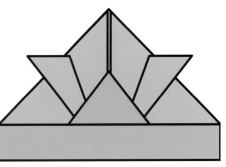

Finished Helmet

MEXICO

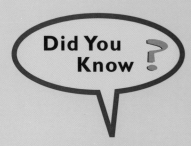

Did You Know?

Most people in Mexico are **Roman Catholics**. When a Roman Catholic child is born in Mexico, he or she is given two names. One of them is a **saint**'s name. The child then celebrates two birthdays each year, one on his or her actual birth date and one on the saint's birthday.

In Mexico and other Latin American countries, the most important birthday party for girls is the Quinceañera (keen-say-ah-NYER-ah), which is a very old tradition dating back to Mexico's **Toltec** and **Mayan** people. When a girl turns fifteen years old, she is given a big party, like a wedding, to honor her **coming of age** as a woman and a future mother.

At other birthday parties, Mexican children enjoy piñatas, which are hollow decorations made of pottery or **papier mâché**. Piñatas come in many shapes, such as animals or favorite characters. They are filled with wrapped candies and tiny toys and hung up as decorations. One by one, party guests are blindfolded and take turns trying to break open the piñata with a large stick or a bat. When the piñata breaks, the candy and toys fall out, and the children rush to gather up the treats.

Popular birthday foods include *Pastel de Tres Leches* (pah-STEL day trays LAY-chays), or Three Milk Cake; *churros* (CHOO-rohs), which are sugar and cinnamon sticks; tacos; tamales; and *atole* (ah-TOH-lay), which is hot, sweet milk.

How to play **Colores**

Mexico is a land of hot sun and bright colors. *Colores* (koh-LOH-rays) is a Mexican game of colors.

You will need:
• six or more players
• a leader (an older child or an adult)
• masks

To make the masks, you will need:
• glue
• heavy paper
• scissors
• string or elastic thread

1 Photocopy the mask patterns on these two pages. Enlarge them, if necessary, to fit your face. Glue the photocopies to the pieces of heavy paper.

2 Cut around the patterns. Ask a grown-up to help you cut out the eyeholes.

3 To hold the mask in place, attach a piece of string or elastic thread that will fit around your head.

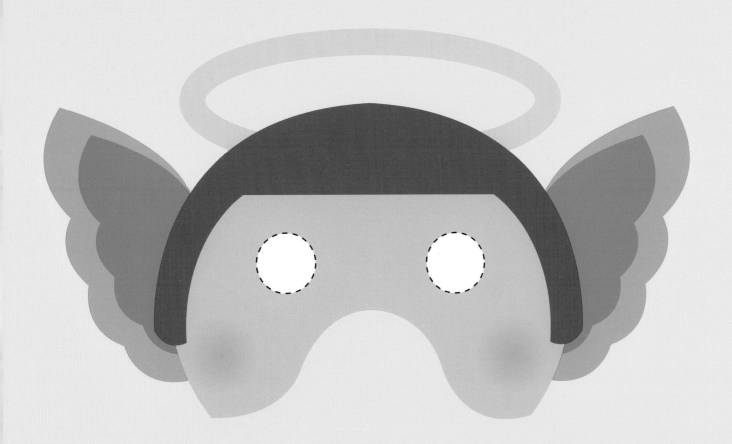

Players sit in a circle on the floor. The leader chooses a devil and an angel and gives each one a mask to wear. They sit with the other players but on opposite sides of the circle. The leader whispers a secret color to each player, except the devil and the angel.

The devil pretends to knock on the leader's door. The leader asks, "What do you want?" The devil says, "A ribbon." The leader asks, "What color?" The devil names a color. The player who has that secret color gets up and runs around the outside of the circle. The devil chases the player. If the player returns to his or her place in the circle without being tagged by the devil, the player is safe. If the devil catches the player, that player joins the devil.

Then the angel knocks on the door, names a color, and tries to catch a player. If the angel catches a player, that player joins the angel.

The devil and the angel take turns until all players have been caught by the devil or the angel. The one who catches the most players wins.

RUSSIA

In Russia, the birthday child celebrates with a pie instead of a cake. A birthday greeting is pricked into the top crust of the pie. *Pirozhki* (peer-OAT-skee), which are dumplings filled with beef, hard-boiled eggs, or cheese and potatoes, are another popular birthday food.

At school, teachers often give small gifts such as flowers, pencils, or books to the birthday child. The gift of books is popular in Russia.

Birthday decorations include fresh or paper flowers and brightly colored place settings. Party favors for guests are pinned to a clothesline.

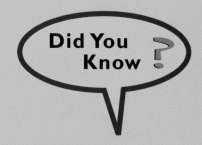

Russian Nesting Dolls

The first *matryoshka* (mah-tree-OSH-kah) was made in 1890. The name comes from a Latin word meaning "mother." A matryoshka is a wooden doll painted cheerful colors. The doll opens to reveal smaller dolls, one tucked inside another. The dolls symbolize motherhood and the connections between generations — and they are fun to play with!

34

How to make a **Party Line**

You will need:
- acrylic paints
- paintbrushes
- clothespins
- a long cord or clothesline
- party favors (such as noisemakers, balloons, paper flowers, and candies wrapped in bright paper)
- ribbons
- blindfold

❶ Paint the clothespins bright colors. Let the paint dry.

❷ Hang a long cord or a clothesline from one side of a room to the other or along a wall.

❸ Clip party favors to the cord with the painted clothespins. Add ribbons for decoration.

❹ Blindfold one guest at a time. Let the guest reach for the party favors. Take turns so that everyone gets a prize!

SOUTH AFRICA

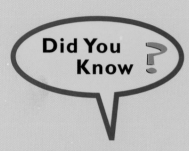
The Zulus have beautiful, complicated dances for different celebrations. Beaded headbands and necklaces, goatskin arm and leg bands, and cowhide shields are all worn for special occasions.

In some native African tribes, such as the **Zulu** (ZOO-loo) and the **Xhosa** (KOH-sah), children's birthdays are not considered very important. Instead, they have special celebrations in their early teen years when they are ready to become adults. These coming-of-age **initiations** are celebrated by people in the child's village.

The many people from India living in South Africa celebrate their birthdays in the Hindu tradition. **Afrikaners**, who have Portuguese, Dutch, French, and British **ancestors**, celebrate birthdays in a European way with gifts and cake. Some of the special foods Afrikaners enjoy include *boerewors* (BOOR-vers), a spicy sausage, and *koeksisters* (KOH-ex-EES-

ters), a sweet, sticky pastry. Other special dishes include a coconut pie called *klappertert* (KLAP-air-tairt) and *sosaties* (soh-sah-TEES), which is marinated lamb or another kind of meat **skewered** with apricots, then grilled. South Africa's mild climate makes outdoor grilling a popular choice for parties.

How to do
Animal Face Painting

For the Xhosa tribe, face and body painting is an important part of traditional celebrations. People are painted as leopards or other animals, from the waist up, using white and red clay. The animals represent a connection with ancestors and the spirit world.

You will need:
- face paints (available in discount stores and some drugstores)
- cold cream or makeup remover
- facial tissues

Face painting is a creative way for people in many parts of the world to "become" animals. With one of these face designs, you can be a leopard, a tiger, or a lion. Use your imagination and create your own animal faces!

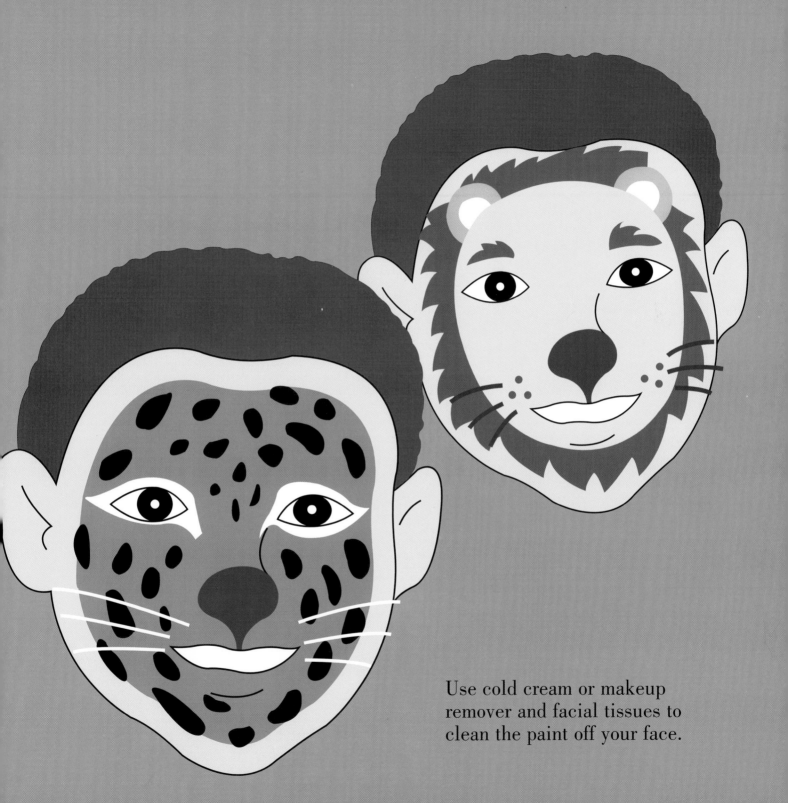

Use cold cream or makeup remover and facial tissues to clean the paint off your face.

41

UNITED STATES

Did You Know ?

The song "Happy Birthday to You" was written in 1893 by two American sisters. This song has been **translated** into many languages and is now sung around the world.

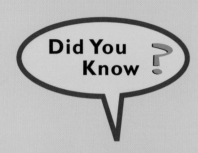

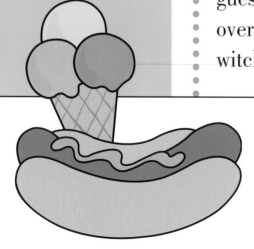

Most children in the United States celebrate birthdays with cakes topped with candles. One candle is placed on top of a cake for each year of the child's life. A cake for a child turning seven years old has seven candles on it.

When the candles are lit, everyone sings "Happy Birthday to You." Then the child makes a wish and blows out the candles. If the child blows out all the candles with one breath, the wish will come true!

Birthday parties with a theme, which means having activities that revolve around a central idea, are very popular. A party with a "pirate" theme might include a treasure hunt. At a camping party, guests could play in a tent and roast marshmallows over a campfire. At a party with a "wizards and witches" theme, children might see a magic show!

Birthday Party Foods

Cake and ice cream are the favorite birthday party foods, but many parties also include a fun meal of hot dogs, potato chips, pizza, and punch or soft drinks before the cake and ice cream.

How to do
The Mysterious Disappearing Leg

You will need:
- a towel, empty pillowcase, or any piece of cloth about 3 x 3 feet (1 x 1 meter)

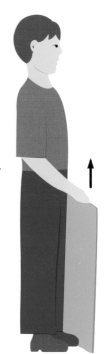

3 After a brief pause, quickly raise the towel back up to waist level. Slowly lower the towel again to hide your feet. Pause, then raise the towel to show your feet again. Nothing has happened.

1 Hold the towel or piece of cloth by two of its corners in front of you. Hold it about waist high so that the bottom hangs down just below your knees. Show both sides of the towel or cloth to the audience so they can see that it is just a normal towel or piece of cloth.

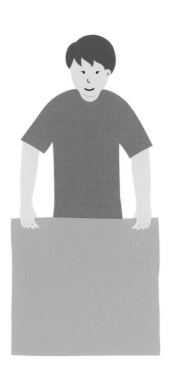

2 Slowly lower the towel until the bottom touches the ground in front of your feet, hiding your feet from the audience.

❹ Slowly lower the towel once more to hide your feet. Then pause again. This time when you raise the towel, slowly bend one leg at the knee to raise one foot off the ground. Keep that leg hidden behind the towel.

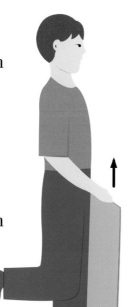

❻ Lower the towel to the ground again, lowering your leg and foot along with it so they stay hidden.

❼ When both the towel and your foot are touching the ground, quickly lift the towel to show the audience that your leg has returned. Take a bow!

❺ To the audience, it will look as if your leg has mysteriously disappeared!

As with any magic trick, be sure to practice this trick in front of a mirror before you try it in front of an audience. When you practice, make sure your leg is showing when it is supposed to be and hidden behind the towel when it is supposed to be. Practicing helps give you confidence and improves your style.

45

Glossary

Aborigines: the earliest inhabitants of Australia

Afrikaners: South Africans of European descent, whose native language is Afrikaans

ancestors: those from whom a person is descended, usually more distant than grandparents

coming of age: reaching an age considered to be adult

immigrants: people who come to a new country to live

initiations: rites or ceremonies through which people become part of a group

karaoke: a device that plays recorded instrumental music for selected songs while people sing the words

marionette: a wooden puppet that moves on strings pulled from above

marzipan: candy made of crushed almonds or almond paste, sugar, and egg whites that is often shaped into fruits, flowers, and other forms

Mayan: belonging to the great civilization of Native people who ruled in Central America from the third century to the ninth century

papier mâché: a mixture of paper and glue that is used to mold shapes

Roman Catholics: members of the Christian church that is headed by the Pope

sacraments: sacred religious acts or ceremonies

saint: a person recognized as holy

Samurai: a warrior in ancient Japan

Shinto: a religion of Japan

shrine: a place devoted to one or more sacred or honored images

shuttlecock: a badminton birdie

skewered: pierced with a thin stick of wood or metal to hold it in place for cooking

symbolize: stand for something else

Toltec: belonging to the ancient people who lived in central Mexico before the Aztecs

translated: changed words from one language into another

Xhosa: a South African tribe that speaks the Bantu language

Zulu: one of the largest existing tribes and oldest cultures in South Africa

More Books to Read

Birthday Rhymes, Special Times. Bobbye S. Goldstein (Bantam Doubleday Dell)

Birthdays Around the World. Mary D. Lankford (HarperCollins)

Births. Ceremonies and Celebrations (series). Jacqueline Dineen (Raintree/Steck-Vaughn)

Celebrating Birthdays in Australia. Birthdays Around the World (series). Cheryl L. Enderlein (Bridgestone Books)

Celebrating Birthdays in Brazil. Birthdays Around the World (series). Cheryl L. Enderlein (Bridgestone Books)

Happy Birthday, Everywhere! Arlene Erlbach (Millbrook Press)

The Perfect Piñata. Kelli Kyle Dominguez (Albert Whitman)

Three Cheers for Catherine the Great. Cari Best (DK Publishing)

Uno, Dos, Tres: One, Two, Three. Pat Mora (Houghton Mifflin)

Yoko's Paper Cranes. Rosemary Wells (Hyperion)

Web Sites

Birthday Traditions Around the World
www.cyberkisses.com/Birthday/birth-traditions.html

Birthday Traditions in Different Countries
www.kidsparties.com/traditions.htm

Cultural Connections
library.thinkquest.org/50055

History of Birthdays and *Birthday Traditions Around the World*
www.birthdayexpress.com/bexpress/planning/BirthdayCelebrations.asp

Traditions from Around the World
www.birthdaycelebrations.net/traditions.htm

Index